Next Level Coaching for Real Estate Professionals

How to Make $100,000+ in Twelve Months in Real Estate

By: Catina R. Willis, MBA

Next Level Coaching for Real Estate Professionals: How to Make $100,000+ in Twelve Months in Real Estate

Next Level Coaching for Real Estate Professionals: How to Make $100,000+ in Twelve Months in Real Estate

ISBN-10: 1979930325
ISBN-13: 978-1979930321
Real Estate: Entrepreneurship

Next Level Coaching

How to Make $100,000+ in Twelve Months
in Real Estate

Who should have this book?

- ✓ New Real Estate Agents

- ✓ New Real Estate Investors

- ✓ Real Estate Agents who feel stuck

- ✓ Aspiring Real Estate Agents

- ✓ New and aspiring Investors who may feel stuck

Table of Contents

Preface

For 20 years, I considered writing a book on various subjects. I thought about writing love novels, books for children, marriage books, or just a plain autobiography. But on August 28, 2017, at Cobo Hall in Detroit, something finally clicked and gave me the push I needed to *just do it*. I was inspired to write this book after attending the Women's Empowerment Expo. My girl, Tiana Von Johnson, was a speaker. She shared so much information to a room packed with women who wanted *increase* in their lives. I realized, there was an abundance of knowledge in my head about the real estate market. I always receive questions from women who want a real estate career like mine. Or men and investors who want to buy and sell like the countless investors I help. I thought to myself, *the time is now*.

Introduction

I want to applaud you for investing in this book and understanding the value of real estate professionals. My real estate career started in 1996 well before I owned any real estate or could even comprehend how impactful it is on the economy. This book will give you some strategies to become successful and build a 6 figure real estate business.

I've spoken to countless agents over time and surprisingly, most say real estate is the most exciting and challenging career they ever had. I will put a spotlight on the triumphs and disappointments most feel the first few years in business.

Many spectators only notice the final results, the glitz, and the glamour of real estate professionals. Unfortunately, it's rare to gain knowledge of what to expect during the learning curves. This book is designed to help you focus and prepare your mindset so that you keep aiming for the next level. Because there is so much to learn and understand when you are new in real estate, this book will show you systems that will minimize mistakes and increase success. I will uncover some of the exact techniques I've used to build and grow my business. Also, disclose my day to day activities.

Next Level Coaching is going to tell some thought provoking stories. You will discover the tough behind-the-scenes efforts too. I simply want to give you pointers so that you can beat the odds and become profitable in an industry where only 20% are considered successful.

Chapter 1
Next Level Blues

As I sat in a real estate office looking timid and feeling confused. I had a flashback of when I quit my stable job after 15 years of employment all because I wanted something more challenging. I daydreamed about the last conversation I had on the telephone with my husband. I would sneak outside for a walk every day and call him to complain and vent about my job. He finally got tired of hearing it and said, "Just quit the damn job, Tina!" That was all I needed was the support of my family. I marched up to the office and typed my resignation letter the same day, though I didn't submit the letter until a week or two later.

I left a good-paying job with no real solid plan. I just knew I craved something more fulfilling. As a newly-licensed real estate agent with nothing to do, I sat there searching online, trying to figure it all out. I noticed some agents in the real estate office appeared to be extremely busy. They would quickly walk past me with a serious look on their face, then go into an office and shut the door. Some would never leave their office or desks. I didn't know what they were doing but I wanted to do it. Most agents didn't really talk to each other. So, I wasn't learning from their conversations either. I shook my head and thought to myself, this doesn't seem half as exciting as I thought it would be. What the heck have I gotten myself into?

My real estate career started in 1997, well before I owned any real estate or even thought much about it. All I had experienced after leaving home at 19 was renting an apartment. After attending a low-income program to gain clerical skills, I found myself to be an extremely fast typist. I got a data entry job at the Realtors Multiple Listing Service. My first job position there was simply to type information into a computer system about the houses. I was later promoted to Customer Care, Training, and Marketing. During the 15 years I worked there, I obtained a bachelor's degree in marketing, and master's degree in business administration. Additionally, I started investing in real estate in 2001. That temporary job turned into so much more than I had ever expected.

After my last position working at the MLS in the marketing department where I advertised and promoted products to real estate agents, I decided my time was up in the real estate field and resigned. I took a month off to figure things out. I later landed a position as an adjunct professor at an art & design school for college students. As we introduced ourselves and spoke of our professional backgrounds, several people asked if I was licensed to sell real estate. I replied "no" and never thought more about it. A few weeks went by and my manager Mr. Kazmi asked if I had ever thought about getting licensed to sell real estate. I wasn't sure what he saw in me, but I had heard this multiple times so thought I would give it a try. I was tired of working Saturdays missing my son's football games anyway and was ready for another change. I went home excited because my husband had talked about getting licensed several times in the past. I asked, "Hey babe, want to go to real estate school?" He was on board. We signed up, and I passed the state exam within 30 days.

So, You Want a Real Estate Career, huh?

Over the years, I've had countless conversations with people who wanted a career in real estate. I always ask, "Why do you want to be in the real estate business?" Most people say, "Oh, I love looking at houses," "It just looks like a fascinating job," or, "I'm good with people and believe I could sell some houses." I always chuckle at these answers because these people have no idea about the hard work completed behind the scenes to make it all happen. In 2017 I attended the Mike Ferry Superstar retreat in Las Vegas. I had a conversation a 23-year-old young man from Detroit name Patrick. He'd just graduated from an engineering program at Michigan State University. I asked him how he'd made a detour into real estate? He replied, "What I like most about real estate is the unlimited earning potential." I smiled. Then he said, "I want to start now in a career that I can turn into a business and pass on to my children." I told this bright young man, "I look forward to seeing your progress, because you get it!"

Have you researched the requirements to become a real estate agent? Sounds simple, doesn't it? You only need to be 18 years old, and don't even need a high school diploma. You sign up for a class that can be taken in two days, two weeks, two months, or online. The class primarily teaches you ethics and legal matters, but doesn't really teach you how to do the job. The real estate course is designed to help you pass the state exam. Once you pass the state exam that consists of 120 multiple choice questions, you will receive a license to sell. (I'll include some secrets to passing the exam in a later chapter.) You might be wondering how so many real estate agents become millionaires with no formal education necessary to get started. The answer is: HARD WORK! However, it CAN be achieved.

Why Real Estate?

In 2014, guidelines for borrowers with student loan debt got more stern. Depending on what a person studies in college, there is a slight chance there may not be a job available after graduation. Comparing college expenses to the investment it takes to build a real estate business is a no-brainer. The first year, you'll pay expenses such as advertising and leads. You'll also pay for coaches and training. A college degree does not guarantee a job, but one thing is certain about real estate: people will always need a place to live.

The average real estate agent makes about $40,000 per year with no college degree required. Based on research from the National Association of REALTORS® 14% of agents make greater than $100,000. 12% of agents make greater than $250,000. That's not too bad especially with many have zero student loan debt. Real estate is a good alternative to college because you learn and grow financially each year.

You Passed the Test Now What?

November of 2012 is when I received my real estate license. I signed up at the real estate office closest to my house, attended all the meetings, but felt discouraged. I thought to myself *I've been assisting licensed agents for more than a decade, I can certainly be successful at this.* With 2013 nearing, I decided to resign from the art school to see where selling real estate could take me if I studied it full time.

In January of 2013, I started as a full-time real estate agent, focusing on it from 9 a.m. to 9 p.m. I went to the office daily, attended all the meetings, bought some leads from **Realtor.com,** and closed my first deal before January 29th. Yes, I closed my first deal within 30 days. I wish all Internet leads were this easy. This buyer just happened to be ready, and had cash. Speaking of internet leads. There's a real art to working with buyers and sellers you meet online. You'll need to ask the right questions to increase success and decrease time wasted.

According to the National Association of Realtors, the average real estate agent closes 8 to 12 deals per year. *And did you know that real estate agents are considered "newbies" until they've experienced more than 4 years of actively selling?*

If you want to be a full time agent immediately and don't already have connections, you may want to interview some leaders of real estate teams or find a reasonable priced real estate coach. Team leaders are groups within a real estate firm that have a business consisting of listing agents, buyer agents, showing agents, assistants, and inside sales associates.

Real Estate Team

Joining a good real estate team is a good way to quickly boost your career. You will likely learn systems and have access to more experienced agents to answer your questions. Systems are the processes successful agents use to continuously generate business and close real estate transactions.

Benefits of joining a real estate team

- ✓ Hands on experience from a top producer

- ✓ Buyer and seller leads given to you

- ✓ You'll make less mistakes

- ✓ You'll learn the business much faster

- ✓ You'll learn systems

Real Estate Coach

A good real estate coach trains you on the business in group settings or one-on-one. A coach may cost $500 to $1,000 per month. However, I have seen coaching as low as $99 per month. Some brokerages offer a coach within a real estate firm and they get paid a percentage once you close a deal. Prices vary, but it's worth it if you need help getting your real estate business started.

Benefits of hiring a real estate coach

✓ **Accountability.** The toughest part about this career is most people believe they're working when they really aren't. A coach helps you understand what income-producing activities are, and what they are not.

✓ **Expertise.** A coach most likely works with a lot of good agents and can give you insight on strategies that work and when to use them.

✓ **Scripts and dialogues.** A real estate coach can provide you with the best scripts and dialogues to use at the right time. I know selling real estate looks simple on television, but there's a real strategy to it.

Becoming a real estate agent is an investment as well as a business. It is not a job, and will not pay you immediately. You should do a lot of research, attend classes, and PUT IN WORK! I was fortunate enough to close 30 transactions my first year. I hired a coach, and was very blessed. GOD wanted me to know that this was where I needed to be.

Coaching Moment

1. Choose a few real estate offices and set appointments with the brokers. Visit at least three to find the best fit for you. I personally like offices that specialize in full service and training. The cap is not important, the value is.

2. Attend seminars a minimum of four times a year. These don't all need to be real estate seminars. Your purpose of being there is to learn and get your business cards in rotation.

3. Talk to everyone you know, and even those you don't know. The reality is that people who know you may not take you seriously as a real estate sales machine yet. You may have better luck finding people to work with you that don't know your past jobs and life challenges.

Goal Setting

Use this section to write 5 goals you wish to accomplish in 5 years. Be specific and write how you will accomplish these goals.

_____

_____

_____

_____

_____

_____

_____

_____

_____

_____

_____

_____

_____

_____

_____

_____

_____

_____

_____

_____

Chapter 2
What to Expect the First Few Years

What should you expect the first year of being a licensed real estate agent? **Plenty of excitement, lots of learning, and tons of emotional roller coasters.**

During the first year you'll discover so much and try to find an area of expertise that fits your personality. You'll learn why there are thousands of active agents in the MLS. You'll also be surprised about the amount of responsibilities completed behind the scenes such as paperwork, negotiations, and client emotions. A major question you'll have is how some agents continuously get new business while others struggle. You'll get different responses from almost every agent you ask. More than likely, you'll try learning as many strategies you can think of to get your real estate business off the ground. My recommendation is to try identifying which specialty or approach is best for your personality type. *For a better understanding of personality types, research DISC, find books about personality types and attend trainings if your office provides it.*

The first 6 months of working full time as an agent, I took a communication course. That is when I learned my personality style was a Driver or Busy Beaver as my first coach called it. Most of that first year was spent reading real estate books, watching videos, and in class. The process was painful at times, but my faith kept me going. I told myself on multiple occasions that I was going to quit the business. You might want to give up too and that's normal. **Just remember good things come to those who hustle!**

Buyers, Sellers, Investors, Oh My

During my first year as a licensed real estate agent, weeks and months quickly flew by. It was challenging to make steady commission checks. I put my heart and soul into working hard to make a difference and understand my finances. With advertising and a bunch of expenses I never had before, my life became somewhat uncomfortable. *The first year I worked with a lot of buyers and made lots of mistakes investing in lead generation tools that did not produce results.* Because I continued to increase my knowledge and skills with coaching and training, I ended up building a reputation and brand people could trust; I also passed out business cards to everyone. That's how business started flowing to me easily and naturally.

Many new agents often don't understand the big difference in working with buyers and sellers. I'll try to summarize it simply. Home buyers are somewhat easy to find because they are time consuming, and agents aren't beating down their door to work with them. Additionally, buyers can be found almost EVERYWHERE. Working with buyers was the biggest shocker to me as a new real estate agent. Buyers are a joy to work with, but most offers do not get accepted the first time; or even the second in a sellers' market.

A seller's market means there are a lot more buyers shopping for a house than there are sellers willing to sell a house. For example, 20 buyers are working with real estate agents waiting to purchase a 2,400 sq. ft. brick house, with 3 bedrooms, 2 full baths, in the same subdivision. Only two houses are currently on the market in this area. That's a seller's market!

The best houses receive multiple offers within days. Before I was a real estate sales agent, I would think one of two buyers would be looking for a specific house in the same area. Offer after offer being rejected taught me to speak up and speak truthfully to buyers who want to submit low ball offers. Talk about a reality check! After gaining more confidence, I recalled a script about low ball offers I learned from my first real estate coach John. I still use it today and it works. Another heart break working with a buyer showing house after house was finally getting an offer accepted, and at the end, they could not get approved for a mortgage, or the appraisal was low, and the deal fell apart. All that time was lost. Nobody pays agents to show properties which is why I recommend having money saved to increase your success factor. The funny thing is, I don't regret any of the headaches I encountered in my humble beginnings. They shaped and molded me to be the person I am today. Full of patience, compassion, integrity, understanding, and EXPERIENCE.

On the other hand, working with sellers is a completely different experience. They are difficult to find but you have a much better chance of getting paid in the end. Working with sellers require advance knowledge and skills. They will ask a lot of questions before deciding to work with you, which is why you need to be ready and prepared. Additionally, when working with sellers, the competition is heavier, the risk is lower, and the experience is always memorable. Your main objective when working with sellers is to learn what to say, make telephone calls, knock on doors, and stay ready!

Finally, let's talk about Investors. This is an interesting bunch. Many locals won't hire you right away because they don't believe they need you. Or they don't believe you have more knowledge than they do. You'll really need advance knowledge and skills to get local investors to trust you and send constant business your way. Just make sure you are working with *real* investors before investing too much time. The main objections I hear from local investors are "I don't need a real estate agent, I can sell the house myself". Or why would I pay you to sell my house, all I have to do is put a sign out." My coaching advice is to know your market prices, study, and become a person so valuable, the client won't be concerned about your commission. When buyers, sellers, and investors see you as someone offering much more than opening a door or putting a house on the MLS, you won't have to worry about who rejects your offer to help them buy or sell. You'll be confident that business will continue flowing in your direction.

My biggest lesson after meeting my first international investor was to always ask for proof of funds. I would advise you not to show multiple properties to any buyer without a pre-approval letter or proof of funds. Most agents get extremely excited and assume the investor is telling the truth. Why would someone fly across the country to buy nothing, right? One of my most memorable real estate incidents was when I met an investor from Singapore who visited Detroit with plans to purchase 30 properties. I was only licensed about 6 months and 30 properties sold meant $30,000 to $40,000 within 30 days. I spent a whole weekend showing him different properties. I submitted about a dozen offers for this investor with a few accepted. A few days later, the investor made it back to Singapore and before he left, he told me to let him know what happens with the other offers, so we can submit more. I was so excited and thankful. Once he made it back home, I received a phone call that he and his company were no longer interested in Detroit because of the bankruptcy announcement few days prior. My heart dropped at the thought of all the time I wasted, and money lost. I chuckle at that situation today and am grateful for it. This experience helped me to quickly identify real buyers from Looky Lous.

Furthermore, as I learned more and grew, I was finally able to connect with serious investors. The kind that respect my knowledge, time, and professionalism. I have 5 to 8 investors who buy and sell properties with me each year or every other year. This is what I love about investors. If you make a good impression the first time, you have a client for life. Real investors are always buying and selling.

Don't Count Your Commissions

Commissions earned and commissions received are two different things. Commissions are a key reason selling real estate can be an emotional roller coaster. I'll just share a few scenarios here of why I advise against counting on a commission - until the day before closing.

Since selling real estate can be such a rewarding career, it also comes with a lot of risks. Sometimes, you'll need to sew a lot of seeds and wait double the expected time for results. However, there will be times during your learning process when you will put in work, and the checks won't come.

Scenario #1: *My first full year in real estate, I had a house pending at $225,000 in November. I thought to myself WOW, that will be a nice holiday check for $6,750. The buyer was pre-approved; I had spoken with his lender, we were all good. The closing date was set for mid-December 16th. A few days prior to closing, we got a message from the lender: "Buyer doesn't qualify for the loan because he failed to mention child support payments." I was very disappointed. A lot of time was lost showing houses, spending 2 hours at the inspection, appraisals, etc. Good thing I had money saved for the holiday.*

Additionally, don't count commissions too early because closings can always get delayed for various reasons. My advice is to **reduce debt, and don't count on a commission too early** if you want to experience a long lasting and rewarding real estate career.

Scenario #2: *I was counting on a commission once and I was double-dipping the transaction. The seller and I spoke by phone daily but then all of a sudden, the calls stopped. Day of closing I called, texted, and emailed. No answer or response. This was a very stressful time for me because the buyer and the lender wanted answers from me. 3 days after the closing date we learned the seller had been hospitalized. The first person he called was me after regaining consciousness. Again, I need to reiterate the importance of having a desire to help people get results. This is the mindset you'll need to succeed. Don't count commissions too early!*

Scenario #3: *I thought I was doing a good deed by helping a good friend of mine get grant money for closing costs and a down payment on a home. She'd been a single mom for 20 years, a typical upstanding citizen. She followed all instructions from her loan officer and attended the first-time home buyer's workshop. Everything was picture perfect, or so we thought. A few days prior to closing, we got a call from the lender saying, "the buyer no longer qualifies for the grant funding because of a bonus check received." This was very heartbreaking for my client and friend. Not receiving the best information from the lender caused her to waste money on appraisals and inspections. Fortunately, my good friend was lucky enough to purchase a better home a year later. Again, I learned:* ***don't count commissions.***

These experiences have shaped me and taught me so much. My motto is: **"Sometimes you win, sometimes you learn!"** There are no losses. Some mistakes are rookie errors, and experienced brokers may identify the signs earlier. The more you learn in this business, the better you get, and the more money you'll make. I'm just grateful for all the lessons learned. I'm still learning every day with each new transaction.

Coaching Moment

1. To continuously generate leads and stay in motion, always ask people who they know that needs to buy, sell, or invest in real estate. Talk to people everywhere you go especially when waiting for a table at restaurants.

2. Buy tee-shirts that say you sell real estate. Be sure to wear them everywhere, especially when working out at the gym.

3. Develop good relationships with trusted loan officers. A good loan officer should communicate in advance that grant funding is not guaranteed. This will prepare buyer to save money for any outcome.

True Story. Don't Be THAT Agent

Stacey is a new agent. She's kind, courteous, and smiles at almost everyone she encounters. She just moved back to Michigan, and doesn't really have connections or contacts. Stacey is hungry to get that first sell, so she starts asking for business on Facebook. She finally gets a decent lead. The buyer was already pre-approved for financing through his credit union, so she started showing him houses. After showing multiple houses, the buyer was ready to submit an offer. The house was listed at $119,000, and Stacey felt it was an unbelievable deal. The buyer wanted to submit the offer at $110,000. Stacey did what he asked her to do. 24 hours later, she informed him that a different offer was accepted. Afterward, he disappeared on her. No returned phone calls or replies to text messages. NOTHING. *He dropped off the face of the earth,* she thought. Two months later, Stacey learned from a friend that the buyer purchased a different house with a different agent.

What could Stacey have done differently? She should have educated the buyer explaining that they were in a seller's market. I always tell buyers submitting an offer lower than the asking price, is likely to be rejected; ultimately giving a different buyer the chance to take the house by submitting a full-price offer. Moral of the story - don't be afraid to tell buyers the possibilities of what may happen if they submit a low-ball offer. It shows you are experienced, and a strong agent. The buyer may have switched agents assuming he didn't get the house because Stacey wasn't effective.

Chapter 3
Explore Real Estate Specialties

There is so much to learn as a new real estate agent, it's impossible to put it all in one book. After passing the real estate exam, you get a real estate sales agent license. The difference between agent and broker is after an agent is licensed more than three years and closed more than 12 real estate transactions, they can take a second exam to become a Broker. After becoming a Broker, you can open an office and allow agents to put their license under your Brokerage. A strategy to passing the test is to take the online practice tests in a quiet place at home, on the computer. Practice exams can be found on mel.org.

Most new real estate agents start off as a **Buyer's agent**. Buyers are easy to find, they are everywhere you go, and they aren't as picky as sellers. A Buyer's agent primarily works with people who are shopping to purchase a house. They earn a commission that's offered by the listing agent on the MLS. A Buyers agent works various hours from sun up to sun down, also on weekends. I remember my first year in real estate working from 9am to 10pm during the summer and even weekends. I was super busy but in a fun way. But I found the business to be exciting, so I woke up each day just to do it again.

Listing agents primarily work with home sellers. Once the seller agrees to work with the listing agent to market and promote the house for sale; they sign an agreement, and this is where the commissions are determined. That commission is usually split 50/50 with the Buyer's agent. Listing agents typically work hours similar to corporate jobs or 9 to 6. They can work later hours at home too. Many of the hours worked are negotiating deals over the telephone or promoting a house online and off. Other primary duties are marketing and promoting the property to other REALTORS. More promotions to get buyers excited about the property, and another significant task of generating new business.

Property Managers primarily handle rental properties. They are responsible for finding and screening tenants, coordinating maintenance repairs, and collecting rent. Property managers consistently make income each week if they are managing a lot of rentals. Property managers typically work 9 to 6 and on weekends. Property managers can also work odd hours and have people on call after hours and on weekends. Many real estate Investor agents are also associated with or own property management companies.

Investor agents primarily work with real estate investors. I personally work with investors from all over the world including places like Israel, China, Argentina, Ireland, California, and Florida. Although, my best investor client is right here in the Detroit area. I met this investor while cold calling. Another real estate agent recommended I start to use a dialing system to make calls. I denied the need for it for 6 months or so. One day when my business was extremely slow I decided to try this dialing system; adding another unwanted expense. The very first week I met a local investor client who is a key player to my success today. Originally this client was skeptical about working with me and drilled me with a lot of questions over the phone. I just remembered all that I was taught by coaches and in training. I could hear Marybeth's voice in my head saying, "all the money is lost in not following up." I followed-up with this client by calling, texting, and emailing, over a two or three week timeframe before earning the business. Today we have successfully sold and closed dozens of properties; and built a winning system. Needless to say, my career is not just about selling real estate. It's about building trusted relationships.

Commercial agents are completely different than residential real estate agents. They typically use a lot of financial information and work with companies to sell or lease. In today's market a commercial deal can still take months to receive a valid offer to purchase and close. A residential property usually receives an offer and the deal gets to the closing table within 40 to 60 days.

Life of a **Luxury real estate agent** is not as glamorous as it may seem. Almost every woman who calls inquiring about a real estate career has the desire to be a luxury agent selling high end properties. When I first started selling, I had the same aspiration until I learned the disadvantages of selling high end real estate. Luxury properties in metro Detroit area generally priced $300,000 and higher. Some take a lot longer to sell than average priced houses at $125,000 to $250,000. Another challenge when selling luxury properties are personality styles. High end clientele is quite different than average clients. One reason is because many are well educated and most do too much research; meaning interview too many agents and get confused. Sometimes people are too educated for their own good and don't want to respect your professional recommendation. Lastly some are complicated just because they have a higher priced property. A number of agents are successful with high end clientele because they naturally have patience and understanding for the clients' concerns. Other agents tell the client what they want to hear about price. Be careful what you wish for. Furthermore, don't stress out if high end properties don't come to you immediately. Unless you have high end connections already, just be patient and it will come as you learn and grow. My coaching advice is to continue doing what works, have fun, and meet lots of new people weekly. You will get to the luxury level when it's your time.

With all these different types of real estate specialties available. And more than 12,000 licensed and active agents in metro Detroit; you might be wondering if there is a place for you in this business. Believe it or not, many agents are part time, some only help family and friends, and others don't work or aren't that good. There is plenty of room if you're determined.

The various real estate agent specialties also lead me to a different thought. "The One Thing" is a book from Gary Keller founder of Keller Williams Realty International. This book describes the success habit we need and what blocks our success. After reading this book, I learned to narrow my focus and that's when I started to elevate myself to the next level. For instance, many new and aspiring agents get licensed and think "I want to be an appraiser and an agent." My advice would to be pick one and become master of it before moving on to something else. I know you're probably thinking "well millionaires have at least 7 streams of income." You too can have multiple streams of income but become a master of one thing first. When I received my real estate license, I first was a buyer's agent. After that, I focused on listings and became a powerful listing agent. Then I expanded to a property management company for my investor clients. After that, I started coaching to help other agents do what I do. All I'm saying is master one thing before you move on to three other things. Otherwise you probably won't be good at anything. ***Grow into doing more.*** Amen'o

So, there you have it. This chapter should have explained why there are thousands of people near major cities licensed to sell real estate. I'd also like you to understand the difference between people who are licensed to sell and agents who actually sell. I speak to dozens of new people each week and some have a bad taste in their mouth after an unpleasant experience with a real estate agent. It's essential to understand the difference in someone who is licensed to sell and someone who is a REALTOR®, a member of the National Association of REALTORS®. A real estate agent may or may not sell but they can show you a license and business card. A REALTOR® is a real estate agent who must uphold the standards of the association and its code of ethics. REALTORS® are also required to take continuing education and legal courses each year.

Additionally, you can also verify an agent by searching their name on the Department of Licensing and Regulatory Affairs (LARA) in your state. This website will tell you if a person has taking continuing education classes, and if the person is active or inactive. Hopefully, this has shed some light and provided a better understanding about the several types of real estate agents.

Coaching Moment

What do Oprah Winfrey, Jim Carrey, and Will Smith all have in common? They swear by using "vision boards." I don't think you can find many successful people who don't put things they want on a vision board. It's simply tangible goals of pictures. You can purchase a board from a dollar store, cut out some pictures or words from a magazine, glue them to your board, and post it somewhere you will view it multiple times a day.

Changing and growing is preparation for the next level. Another way to grow is to surround yourself with positive people and those who are doing well. My past coach Sherry always reminds us, you are the average of the five people you hang around most. If your circle doesn't look promising, change it!

1. Growth starts outside of your comfort zone. This means you must do something different. If you normally go to the park on Saturday, go to a different park, take an exercise class or a self-development course, or even take on a new hobby.

2. Volunteer work is a wonderful way to meet new and interesting people. Volunteering also helps you learn new systems and business models. If you are feeling stuck in life and your place of employment has no room for growth, learn more about volunteer work. A few great places you can volunteer are: church, retirement homes, real estate offices, political campaigns, or art museums.

3. Put your goals and vision in writing today. Go to the dollar store, get a journal or notebook and write all your real estate goals and dreams in it. Each time you have an idea, write it down. TAKE ACTION!

What's your Specialty?

Use this section to write the type of real estate agent you'd be good at and why. Also, write goals and a plan of action that will help you grow to be the best you can at this specialty.

_____

_____

_____

_____

_____

_____

_____

_____

_____

_____

_____

_____

_____

_____

_____

_____

_____

_____

_____

_____

_____

_____

_____

_____

_____

_____

Chapter 4
If you're not Growing, You're Dying

I once called Outback Steakhouse to place a carry-out order. I was told they were so swamped they couldn't take any carry-out orders. I thought to myself *hmm, that's very strange that a company would throw away business*. I've been calling this same Outback restaurant for years, so I'm wondering what has changed. Then, I remembered they started a delivery service. I could be wrong, but maybe that's part of the problem. The company added a service, but probably didn't give the cooks and other employees any additional incentive or resources to push out more orders. That led me to smile about the beauty of the real estate business. When you grow and increase production by adding additional services, you WILL receive additional pay for your efforts. The more work you do, the more you get paid in the real estate business. It's your decision! In 2015, I decided to work 90 days straight during the summer months-no days off-and that's when I finally had a breakthrough. In this business, it's all on you. You can decide to make $25,000, $100,000 or $1 million. It's based on your production, performance, drive, and systems.

My First Million-Dollar Listing

There are so many wonderful things about the real estate profession. One of the reasons I love this profession is the unlimited opportunities and open doors. The best part for me is constantly meeting new and interesting people. Some of these people may become part of your life forever. You will also encounter some difficult people who will challenge the hell out of you too. Nonetheless, be kind to everyone you meet. Treating people with kindness should happen naturally for most good human beings. I'm simply reminding you because it will increase your level of success. This leads me to a story about my first million-dollar listing. I was listing a house for $20,000 on the west side of Detroit. This was when the market was all the way down. I met with the owners to take interior pictures. The plumber was there installing a hot water tank. I chatted with him for a few minutes and handed him my business card. Some months later, the plumber called me to say his aunt owns 50-plus properties, and he wanted to know if it was ok to pass my contact information along to her. "Of course," I said, "SURE, please do, with a big smile on my face. I met with his aunt and was selected to list the family's high profile, unique listing. This opportunity landed me a lot of unexpected free publicity. I was interviewed by several real estate news journalists, mentioned in several newspaper articles, and on the news multiple times. Talk about getting connected and networking!

I did not sell that million-dollar listing, but I'm grateful for the experience and opportunity. I believe I am still reaping the benefits from all that publicity to this day. This is the reason you treat every client like family, a friend, or a million bucks!

TELL THE WORLD...Don't Be a "Secret" Agent

Based on the million dollar listing story, you probably now realize how important it is to tell everyone you meet that you sell real estate. This really will help you go to the next level. I speak with a lot of new agents who feel stuck and frustrated. Some say, "I don't like social media," "I don't want to do this," and "I don't want to do that. Don't be embarrassed about your new venture. Growth starts outside of your comfort zone, tell the world about your real estate business. Social media enables you to send one message to thousands of people within seconds. Most social media marketing is free.

Just because family members and long-time friends only know you as little Susie or Tim-Tim doesn't mean you can't grow up. TELL THE WORLD when you get licensed! Otherwise, people will never know. Nor can they send business to you. Approximately 60% of my business is repeat clients or referrals. I love referrals! Some people promote me just as well as I would promote myself. Don't get me wrong, I'm not saying they will all support you; some will, and some will not. Some people want to see your growth before allowing you to help them buy or sell real estate. Additionally, don't get upset if family or neighbors don't choose you. They just don't want you to know all their business. GROWTH!

What does your Online Brand say about you?

Have you googled yourself lately? What people see or hear about you when googling your name is the brand you've created. Many homeowners will Google an agents name before deciding to hire them. Be mindful of what you share publicly on social media. So exactly how can you sell real estate using Facebook, Twitter, and Instagram? Well, first you'll need to brand yourself as a real estate expert. Show, don't sell! Don't be that agent who consistently asks for business. Simply post meaningful content such as pictures of houses, sales statistics, or photos of you and your clients. Start early establishing yourself as someone who knows real estate. Let your audience know everything you're learning and working on. You can post information about neighborhoods, news articles, or just talk about sale prices. But most importantly, as soon as you are licensed, post a picture of the test results that say "PASSED." Next, you should share a picture of your business card. The sky is the limit after that.

Mindset

Life is like an elevator ride. Some people close to you will need to get off the elevator before you make it to the top. Be at peace with that. This common sense to some, but you must take extra care of your mindset. People will tell you to quit real estate if you aren't making any money immediately. Selling real estate takes time for some people. The seeds must be planted before your business flourishes.

To increase success, have 3 to 6 months income saved. Real estate sales is a business, and you must treat it as such. Take it seriously if you want to make serious money. Don't go into real estate just because the schedule allows flexibility. Most learn quickly that a relaxed schedule will produce irregular dividends. A consistent schedule produces a more reliable income.

Selling real estate is a career in which you NEVER stop learning. You will get better and better. The job will get easier and easier, and you must believe that. This is a business in which you need to be a person of faith.

Protecting your mindset includes controlling what you watch on television. The news rarely reports the number of people who traveled to work and made it home safely without getting into a car accident or getting shot. The news always reports a deadly car accident, people fighting, or any other violent acts you can think of. People love to spread negative news. Just scroll through your Facebook timeline. 9 out of 10 people will report violence for the negative news stations. Protect your mind set, and try staying away from gossip and negative news stories. This helps you stay upbeat and optimistic.

Again, have 3 to 6 months of income set aside for monthly bills and expenses. This business requires time, patience, and a plan.

Some people say, "No new friends." If you're in real estate, though, you won't think that. You'll notice some people dropping out of your life like flies, and others coming in.

If you feel stuck in your job and don't believe you'll have any friends or family left once you start making moves in real estate, you're probably right. If you believe your real friends and loving family will be right there by your side, you're probably right about that too. What I'm saying is, whatever you believe will likely happen. This is called "the law of attraction."

Want to learn another shock factor to expect as a new real estate agent? You'll get used to rejection. Almost everyone will reject your service-even friends and family. It might become discouraging because you may experience friends or family choosing a different real estate agent as you haven't proven yourself yet. To fight back, you'll need to SHOW people that you are well-qualified.

Life is short. Get started and take action. Don't be afraid to leave friends behind, and don't feel you cannot do something without friends or family there to help. GOD, the universe, or whatever faith you have will guide you; just take the first step.

A few years ago, after losing some friends and a spouse, I started saying affirmations. I believe it helped me become a cheerful and more optimistic person. Affirmations are positive statements that rewire our brains. Basically, you speak positively about your life to condition your subconscious. The goal is to attract more happiness and positivity.

Read the following affirmations out loud. You can also create your own.

- ✓ I am creative.

- ✓ I am smart and beautiful.

- ✓ My soul attracts the most positive people.

- ✓ I am the best salesperson.

- ✓ The best buyers and sellers hire me.

- ✓ Serious buyers need me.

- ✓ I am brave.

- ✓ I am a winner.

- ✓ Motivated sellers love for me to sell their house.

- ✓ I am loved.

- ✓ I'm the greatest real estate agent in Detroit.

- ✓ My business is growing and expanding daily.

- ✓ I am blessed with loving friends and family.

- ✓ "I'm a money magnet, money naturally flows to me." (This is my favorite affirmation from KW Bold.).

Coaching Moment

1. Listen to something positive in the morning instead of the news. Try spiritual music, meditation, or something that makes you laugh.

2. Try exercising in the morning. Even if it's only a 10 minute walk, jumping jacks, or stretch. This will energize you and help you feel more upbeat.

3. Call or post on social media. Ask who they know that wants to sell or buy real estate. Ask a minimum of 15 people every day. Periodically, you should also tell them you are in a contest at work. Be creative!

4. Post pictures on social media informing your audience of what you're learning and working on. Also, record and post videos to YouTube.

True Story. Don't Be THAT Agent

Jerry is a brand-new real estate agent. He had worked in the entertainment business most of his adult life, and didn't take himself seriously as an agent. Yet, he attended classes and seminars to better prepare himself.

Fast forward 3 months after Jerry earned his real estate license. Jerry's daughter tells him she's sad her best friend is moving an hour away. Jerry immediately asks where and why? The daughter doesn't know much, so when Jerry drops his daughter off at her best friend's house, he decides to do something he ordinarily would not and have a conversation with the best friend's mother. He asks why are they moving and how did it happen so fast. The best friend's mom tells Jerry, "A real estate agent posted the recent sold price of a house in my area. A friend shared it with me on Facebook. The mom had been thinking about moving, so she gave the agent a chance when she saw how much she could sell the house for. The house sold in three days for $220,000. Jerry was surprised and congratulated her. However, he was a little disappointed for not promoting himself.

Don't be a "secret" agent. Jerry lost $6,600 to $13,000 all because he didn't tell anyone about his new career.

Take time to write down how to best promote yourself on social media. Think of the brand you want to create for yourself.

_____

_____

_____

_____

_____

_____

_____

_____

_____

_____

_____

_____

_____

_____

_____

_____

_____

_____

_____

_____

Affirmations

Take some time to write your own personal affirmations. Look in the mirror and say them daily.

Chapter 5
Next Level Path and Math

Earning $100,000 in the real estate business is not a big deal for many in this industry. However, it is a milestone, and many agents are happy to reach it. Here are a few ways to earn $100,000+ as a real estate agent:

- Get 3 to 5 new listings each month that can sell for $125,000 or more. This is a piece of cake in certain markets. You only need to close 3 a month.

- Find 2 to 4 willing-and-able buyers each month who want to buy a house for more than $150,000.

- Find 1 to 3 real estate investors who want to sell 5 or more properties each month. These can be lower priced properties - just make sure the commission is a minimum of $2,500 for each one you sell.

- Find 1 to 3 investors (in your state or a different state) who are willing to purchase 3-5 or more properties.

Pass out business cards to EVERYONE. Even when you're at social events or restaurants. Just introduce yourself and ask them who they know that needs to buy, sell, or invest. You can only grow by getting comfortable with being uncomfortable.

The Formula to earn $150,000

	The Basic Formula for the Economic Model of the MREA						
		CAP BY MAY 2016					
	For Sellers	Monthly			**For Buyers**	Monthly	
	66.43 Seller Listing Appointments	5.54			47.98 Buyer Listing Appointments	4.00	
	80% % Conversion Rate		x		75% % Conversion Rate		
	53.14 Seller Listings Taken	4.43	=		35.98 Buyer Listings Taken	3.00	
	65% % Conversion Rate		x		80% % Conversion Rate		
x	34.54 Sellers Sold		=		28.79 Buyers Sold		
=	125,000.00 Average Sales Price		x		150,000.00 Average Sales Price		
x	4,317,789.29 Seller Sold Volume		=		4,317,789.29 Buyer Sold Volume		
=	3.0% % Commission		x		3.0% % Commission		
x	129,533.68 Gross Revenue from Sellers		=		129,533.68 Gross Revenue from Buyers		
=	50%				50%		
		259,067.36	Total Gross Revenue or GCI			Assume 42.1%	
		- 109,067.36	Expenses/Cost of Sales			Expenses 12.9%	
		= 150,000.00	Net Income			Cost of Sales 29.2%	

Courtesy of Keller Williams International

*Cap by May 2016 indicates when the agent wants to finish paying the real estate company. The price to pay a company varies

Real Estate Expenses 2016

	Monthly Cost	Yearly Total
Advertising	$ 199.00	$ 2,388.00
MLS and Board Fees		$ 1,147.00
Meals		$ 300.00
Office Fees	$ 100.00	$ 1,200.00
Travel & Education		$ 2,300.00
Phone	$ 150.00	$ 1,530.00
Internet	$ 30.00	$ 360.00
Gas	$ 160.00	$ 1,920.00
Mailings and Postage		$ 320.00
Business Cards and Post Cards		$ 400.00
Client gifts and dinners		$ 1,800.00
Custom Signs and Install		$ 295.00
Office Supplies		$ 150.00
Total	$ 639.00	$ 13,665.00

This table indicates what expenses may look like for a real estate agent who earns $100,000 or more each year.

"6-Figure" Master Techniques

Door knock – Go to neighborhoods, knock on doors, and ask them when they plan to move. Ask if you can email them real estate updates. Stay in touch and become their go-to person.

Start blogging – Write about neighborhoods or cities you like. Become an expert on specialties such as Luxury Homes or Investment Properties.

Treat each client like a Million Bucks – Sometimes it may be difficult, but if you cater to clients, they will think you are the best, and they will send you more business.

Layered Open House – Ask a top agent in your office if you can host an open house at one of their listings. This will help you connect with buyers. You'll meet sellers as well. A Layered Open House involves calling everyone in the neighborhood to invite them to the open house. Also, knock on doors and leave your flyer. This helps you to have conversations with homeowners in the area. You may also get lucky and meet a buyer who wants to purchase the house you're showing, or a different house.

Social media presence – Show your social media followers and friends on Facebook, Instagram, or LinkedIn what you do. They WILL start to send you business. I'm always pleasantly surprised when someone on social media reaches out to me with a referral. Ironically, it's usually someone who has NOT been clicking "like" on my posts.

Business-to-business referrals. Visit your local State Farm or AAA insurance company. Tell the salesperson you will direct clients to them if they will refer potential real estate clients to you.

Coaching Moment

1.   Go to the office daily, or at least 4 times a week to call or job shadow. During the afternoons, show houses, preview houses, or go to networking events.

2.   Ever heard the motto, "Surround yourself with the best and you will become the best," or "Iron sharpens iron?" As I stated before, real estate is a tough business and you will need support and smart people around you in your personal and professional life.

3.   Get a coach. A good real estate coach can jumpstart your career. Providing guidance, scripts and dialogues, and action plans to generate business.

Chapter 6
Mo Money, Mo Problems

If I could name 2017 a chapter in a book, it would be called: "The Year of Lawyers, Judges, and Haters." My son told me that title sucks, and "Mo Money, Mo Problems" was a better fit. Diddy was right! As people see you progressing and selling more real estate monthly, they will come for you. Whether they have a valid reason to or not. They will want what they think you have, without doing what you did to earn it. Isn't that interesting?

I simply want to pay off my student loans, invest, take a few vacations, save some money, and love loyal people. Don't give your enemies your energy. But don't totally ignore them either, like I did.

What Can You Expect on Your Way to the Top?

Some people will walk out of your life. This is a part of growing - be ok with it. The right people will still be there when you do make it.

All the pain and everything you will experience is part of the process. It's OK To let some people go. They're just making room for the right people. Spend some alone time. Then get around the right people, and live the fruitful life that you desire so deeply in your heart. Enough ranting about personal issues I've experienced. Back to the subject at hand. You can certainly bet on experiencing more problems when selling high end properties. The clients tend to be a lot more challenging and sometimes emotional. What I've noticed is most people in the Detroit area who are selling property above $300,000 are more educated and some may think they know more than you about real estate. When helping luxury buyers and sellers, make sure you know your stuff and be sharp. Just a few weeks ago, an agent came into my office to tell me a story about her client and friend of many years who didn't want to pay her 3% on a property priced above $450,000. She sold the property too fast the seller thought. Basically, the client didn't believe the agent earned $13,500. This home seller challenged the agent all the way until day of closing. Be ready!

Higher priced properties are also a problem because the owner will likely interview multiple agents. They will have you visit the house multiple times, forcing you to sell yourself again and again, bring all sorts of statistics, and tell you over and over how unique their property is. Just to possibly choose someone else of the 10 agents they have interviewed. In many instances, luxury homeowners, put you through the ringer, and the properties take longer to sell. Real estate investors can be very demanding also. They force you to raise the bar. Many successful investors are very unemotional and detached. They don't care about anything except the numbers.

Real Estate Agent Conclusion

So now you've heard the good, the bad, and the ugly as a real estate sales agent. After a few months in real estate, so many agents ask, "why am I still doing this?" What do I really like about this business? My coaching advice is to keep going if you really want it. Nothing good comes easy. If you don't give up, you will receive rewards in abundance and continuous opportunities.

It took approximately 3 to 4 years for me to produce the results I craved. This took a lot of training, coaching, hard work, dedication, being surrounded by the right people, and faith. That's about the same time frame it takes to complete a college degree, right?

Remember, everyone is on their own journey so don't compare yourself to others. I'm not saying don't study your competition, but don't be discouraged if they get faster results than you do. Remember, **It's You against YOU every day**. Your goal should be developing yourself each week, month, and year.

Life as a real estate professional has been rewarding for me. I believe I'm more successful than the average real estate agent because I learn, I'm passionate about helping others, and dedicated. I always tell my 16 year old son that selling real estate is not about the money, it's about solving someone's problem. He laughs so hard each time I tell him this. I really believe when you help someone else reach their goals, you're bound to achieve your own goals. Think BIG, take action, and Have Patience! Set high standards for yourself and trust the process! Then you will be on your way to the Next Level.

Chapter 7
My Real Estate Niche: INVESTING

I sat in a restaurant going back and forth with my friend James about an investment section of the book. He believed investing should be in a completely different book. As I chewed my salad and sipped red wine, I told him real estate investing is my heart. I was an investor for many years before gaining a real estate license. I *must* talk about investing in my first real estate book.

My real estate investment journey started in 2001. I had a 3 month old baby, and I started purchasing properties to create passive income. Back then (before the market crashed in 2007), it was much easier to finance a house and pay $300 to $400 per month on the mortgage. We would rent the same house for $800 plus per month. Before I knew it, my team owned about a dozen rentals in Detroit. It was FANTASTIC; I quickly felt the fever.

What I love most about real estate investing is a person can create positive cash flow with knowledge and research. Just find a discount property that can rent high. One investor I know always says, "Buy the worst house in the best neighborhood, and you'll never go wrong." It will take some work a.k.a. rehab, but it will pay off later with good cash flow. In today's Detroit market, you can find a brick house in a decent neighborhood for approximately $30,000 to $40,000, make the necessary repairs, and rent it for $800 plus per month. That's $9,600 per year, and approximately a 15% to 20% return on your investment. Sounds simple, right? Real estate investing is special to me, not only because it's fascinating. I just always feel so blessed when a new investor puts all their trust in me to help with such an important transaction. In some instances, their funds are linked to their retirement.

What's the difference between a successful and an unsuccessful real estate investor?

I work with investors who have millions in the bank, and I meet local investors who tell me they tried investing, but didn't like it. The reason they didn't like it is because they didn't have a plan or system in place. In many cases, unsuccessful investors were tight on funds, and moved the first person into the house who had a security deposit.

I've encountered countless people who can't wait to tell me their horrific stories about trying to become a real estate investor. Most read an article or two online and decided to dive in rather than get information from a licensed, good, experienced broker who specializes in investments. If you're not willing to seek free advice from credible people, you're bound to make a mistake or two. Real Estate Investments remains a higher return for your money than stocks and bonds. That is, if it's done right.

September 2017, Detroit was named fifth hottest real estate market, according to the New York Times. The rankings are based on how long listings take to sell on the Realtor.com website. With pricing still historical low, why aren't more people who live in Detroit investing?

See the chart below which explains.

SUCCESSFUL INVESTOR TRAITS	UNSUCCESSFUL INVESTOR TRAITS
Very selective about the house	Not picky about the house, only price
Makes location a priority	Will buy as long as it's cheap
Stays educated	Knows it all
Builds a network	Doesn't want to pay commissions
Screens tenants thoroughly	Rents to the first applicant with money

Knowledge is Power

Did you know that the best investment deals are not found on the MLS? Seriously, good deals are everywhere; people just don't ask for them. **The best deals are usually sold off market and found by prospecting, or communicating with friends and neighbors.** If you want to be an investor, create business cards and start having conversations with people. Tell them to call you if they hear of someone who needs to sell a property.

Know Your Numbers

Serious and experienced investors seek expert advice about what a property can sell for PRIOR to purchasing it. I work with a wholesaler who emails me to run comps before he initiates a cash offer. This gives additional support to help them make an educated offer. Experienced investors always want a professional opinion of what the property is worth before purchasing. Since Detroit has "good" rental prices, the two most important ratios investors want to know are the cap rate and ROI. Cap rate tells how much a property earns each month. Return-on-Investment (ROI) indicates the total return.

I met my first investor immediately after receiving my real estate license and working full-time. I had been investing since 2001 and owned three rental properties at the time. I decided to put them on the market to see how the process of being a listing agent worked. Instantly, I attracted investors from Singapore and Ireland. The investor from the Ireland eventually purchased more than 11 properties in Detroit and its surrounding suburbs.

You might be wondering why so many investors from California, Florida, Argentina, Tokyo, Taiwan, Singapore, and United Kingdom are watching Detroit. **A few cities in South East Michigan including Eastpointe, Warren, Redford, Southfield, and Detroit have been noticed as places with the best return on investment.** Investors flock to these areas to purchase properties in bulk and to grow their portfolios. Additionally, turn-key properties in Michigan are more affordable than most states. Metro Detroit return rates are typically 18% to 25%.

Rookie Investor BIGGEST Mistakes

Location, Location, Location! Yes, investors, this applies to you, too. People who make a living investing in real estate always buy in desirable locations. Values tend to increase faster if a property sits in a good area.

I'll give a quick example of why it's important to purchase your investment property in the right location: one investor called to sell his property. He purchased a brick house for less than $7,000 when the Detroit market was all the way down. He invested an additional $20,000 into the property he told me. Unfortunately, this investor never contacted an experienced real estate broker to see comps or even ask for a professional opinion. By the time the investor came to me, I had to break the sad news. The property was located in a bad location. Across the street sat a big blue factory. Also, the house was approximately 1,000 square feet. Smaller houses are primarily sold to investors for renting purposes. He was hoping to sell retail to a first time home buyer for $60,000. I had to explain how appraisers put a value on a property and use recent "solds" in the area. He had invested more money into that house than the house was worth. *Remember, the whole point of investing in real estate is to resell the property later-after values increase.*

Cheaper Doesn't Indicate Better Deal

During the down market, we saw some ridiculous prices in Detroit. Houses were being sold as low as $500 and even $1. Today,

I get calls periodically from someone wanting to purchase a house for $5,000. Of course, I ask them if they want to purchase a cheap house just to put $30,000 into it. It's strange, but these are important details new investors may not consider. Get an agent who will be up front and honest about the cost down the line. If you want to grow and increase success.

Quality not Quantity

Need I say more? If your mind is telling you to buy a long-term investment where you get good tenants who pay on time, buy a quality property. *What is a quality property?* Quality properties are located in neighborhoods that look clean with manicured lawns. Find neighborhoods that consist of working class people. Don't get me wrong, you can find a great cash-flowing property when purchasing in a less desirable neighborhood too. Just get a section 8 tenant to receive top rental dollar. Knowing what to buy and where is critical!

Leverage...TEAM UP

Once you understand leverage, you will likely experience an INCREASE: increase in income, business opportunities, and time to think and create more wealth. Rookie thinking will tell you that working with an agent takes money out of your pocket. Experienced investors know that building a relationship with a licensed real estate broker can bring more opportunities their way. Remember, they talk to buyers and sellers daily. Instead of posting a bunch of "We Buy

Houses" signs, develop a good relationship with someone who can bring good deals to you.

Buy and Hold, or Flip

There are various kinds of real estate investors, and the two most common in the Detroit area are house flippers, and investors who buy and hold. Which type of investor do you want to be? Let's talk about the buy and hold first. Investors who prefer rentals will purchase the property to collect rent for a few years until the house appreciates in value. A house flipper will purchase a property with the intent of selling it immediately. Some investors choose to rehab and modernize the property nice for a home owner. While other investors may improve the house a little bit and sell to a different investor. **My personal favorite is to "fix and flip."** My flipping strategy is to talk to as many people as possible to discover if they have a property to sell and want it sold quickly. Some places to find these types of people are: divorce courts, probate courts, and back property tax lists. Many investors I work with from other parts of the US and overseas are planning to buy and hold. They want to rent the property for a few years, then purchase bigger-priced investments later.

Benefits of buy and hold

1. Build Equity as the property appreciates in value.
2. Positive cash flow.
3. Tax advantages.

Benefits of House Flipping

1. Quick Cash - some house flippers benefit financially in 30 to 90 days depending on the project.
2. Less Risk - Many house flippers go this route to get in and get out fast. Some people still feel the pain of the real estate crash of 2007. This may be an attempt to reduce risk.
3. Tenant Pain - No tenant headaches or continuous repair issues.

Types of Deeds

Now let's talk about one of the most common issues I run into with Detroit properties purchased from the tax foreclosure auction Many investors purchase a property and have no idea what they are getting. Normal property sales provide a Warranty Deed. However, the tax foreclosure sale provides a **Quit Claim Deed**. There is a big difference between the two. Additionally, anyone who buy properties directly from the owner is usually offered a quit claim deed. Home sellers offer this to eliminate paying for title insurance and because it's easier to gain the documents and close the deal. Unfortunately, this can cause problems for the new owner in the future. Furthermore, a home seller could offer a quick claim deed because they have complications with the title. They know hiring a real estate agent and using a title company may expose the truth. *Always hire a professional when buying real estate.* It is very important that you understand what you are purchasing. The whole point of investing in real estate is to sell for a higher profit later, correct? **A quick claim deed contains no warranty**. Basically, the seller can transfer and sell a property to you using this type of deed, but that does not guarantee there are no liens on the property. A general warranty deed or special warranty deed is your best bet. This is when a title insurance company is involved, and their warranty promises that the grantee or seller had title insurance. It also warrants against any claim against the title. If anyone makes a claim to the property (even years prior) he the grantor of the warranty deed is responsible for the issue. *Warranty Deed is your best choice when purchasing real estate.*

Everybody knows a Real Estate Agent

Did you know that more than half the licensed REALTORS® in each state sell less than 15 properties in twelve months? Therefore, when someone tells me their cousin or even wife is an agent, I might chuckle and have a great objection to that. Almost everyone knows a real estate agent, but you should be strategic when you work with to sell your important investment. Find an agent who sells the type of properties you are buying. Find the type of broker who's experienced and is actually SELLING. Trusted and reliable real estate professionals and contractors are extremely important also when you are a house flipper. Start building relationships now, and get to know people - see their work. Additionally, a valuable partner will help you increase success with your real estate investment business. You need a partner who can help you think strategically, has skills and expertise, and contributes financially is a big benefit too. Work with a good and thorough title companies that'll assist you in closing the transactions.

Coaching Moment

1. What do you need to increase success in real estate investing? First thing to do is connect with an experienced team of people with a good reputation and creative strategies. The first person I suggest is a real estate broker. I find it is so amusing when people tell me, "Oh, my cousin's a real estate agent" or "My friend's a real estate agent, I don't need an agent." And they wonder why their business is not thriving.

2. Always ask a professional and actively working real estate agent to provide a market analysis when you invest. In an area where houses are selling between $15,000 and $25,000, it doesn't make sense to buy a home for $5,000 if it needs $15,000 or more in rehab. If this property was located in an area where houses were selling above $60,000, the sale and rehab amounts would work. **Always consider rehab costs and market values!**

3. Ask and understand the type of deed you are getting when purchasing a house. Especially if buying from seller directly. If you purchase from an auction, you may need to hire an attorney to perform **Quiet Title Action**.

How to Become a Flipper

Flipping is the most fun part of real estate investing, in my opinion. You find a house that needs work (a.k.a. an ugly frog), and turn it into a beautiful palace for a princess. So, how can this be accomplished? Find motivated sellers! "Motivated" means someone experiencing the following hardships:

- ✓ Divorce

- ✓ Death in the family

- ✓ Job transfer

- ✓ Tired of tenants because they don't have a team

- ✓ Personal issues/Freeloading relatives

- ✓ Financial problems

- ✓ Tax Liens/Foreclosure

These are the most common problems that will indicate how motivated a seller is. In many instances, they just want to get rid of a property. You'll need to make lots of telephone calls, knock on hundreds of doors, post plenty of "We Buy Houses" signs-or team up with an experienced, licensed real estate Investment broker.

How to Find Good Flips

In today's seller's market, most good flips are not found on the Multiple Listing Service. I'll help you explore some of the best ways to find a good flip:

- ✓ **Tax auctions**. These are foreclosed properties in which a property owner lost the house for unpaid property taxes.

- ✓ **Probate sales**. The property owner may have died without a will and the probate court has to approve the sale. Normally these houses are below market value.

- ✓ **Join a real estate investment group.** Many of these members are wholesalers or own multiple properties.

- ✓ **Connect with divorce and bankruptcy attorneys.**

- ✓ Establish a relationship with a **real estate investment broker** who works with multiple investors.

Wholesalers

There is absolutely no way we can talk about house flipping without mentioning wholesaling. The wholesale agent is very similar to listing agent, but *some* are not licensed and don't have too many rules. Let's use a scenario to make this information more transparent: a wholesaler will post marketing and advertising to find a deal or a motivated home seller. The home seller may want to sell the property for $100,000 in its "As Is" condition. The wholesaler researches the property and learns that after spending $15,000 in repairs, the house may be able to sell for $199,000. The wholesaler gets the house under contract for $90,000. The homeowner walks away with cash and free of the problem making repairs they could not afford. Pretty good house flip, don't you think?

Real Estate Investor Path

Much like a real estate career, investors who want to make *$100,000* within twelve months will spend time doing the following: talking to people, using lead generation systems and software, sending mailers.

A few techniques to use for finding motivated sellers today: obtain real estate foreclosure lists or emails, search tax and auctions online, and visit probate or divorce courts. Additionally, connect with a good real estate broker who specializes in investments. This person should be able to send leads to you as well.

Best Strategies to Find Motivated Sellers

Referrals are still the best way to get business. Build a trusted reputation, get professional business cards, and tell all your friends and family to notify you if someone needs to sell a property quickly. This is the quickest, yet most painless way to find motivated sellers. Lead generation software is a good method for finding motivated seller also. You simply call people and ask if they are thinking about selling a property. If they say *yes*, learn their motivation. Additionally, use flyers and door hangers to promote your business. Just like real estate agents, pound the ground and go talk to people. Pass out your business card in areas of interest. Just be prepared, study the market, and know your numbers, in case someone calls.

How Much Can You Really Make as a
Real Estate Investor?

Honestly, the sky is the limit based on each individuals' resources, drive, and determination. One key reason I see beginner investors fail is they don't budget properly. I always advise investors to keep money to the side for rehab and unpredicted issues. Typically, a house that has sat for months or years will need some repair that is not immediately visible to the eye. For example, there could be an unknown plumbing problem or tree root issue if nobody has lived in a house for a while. There's almost always more to do. Additionally, budgeting improperly could cause an investor to get desperate and accept the first tenant who has money. The rich and experienced investor take tenant screenings very seriously. They know that the wrong tenant, in the end, can cost. Experienced investors will keep their property vacant and go through dozens of people before collecting a security deposit, down payment, and then turning over keys.

Another reason some investors are successful while others aren't is they know when to get out. Studies show that the real estate market changes about every 7 to 10 years. *Know when to hold and know when to fold* as my client Vinh always says.

What's your Next Level?

Surprise! You've already gone to the next level by reading this book, congratulations. If you want to be a real estate investor or an agent, I hope you gained some ideas and expanded your real estate knowledge by reading this book.

Earning $100,000 is small peanuts for some real estate professionals. I thought it was important to speak to those who are aiming for six figures right now. We all started, somewhere right?

So, what are the next steps? You should complete a few very important tasks right now.

- Put specific goals in writing and keep them in plain sight. People who write their goals down are more likely to achieve them.
- Put a vision board together and hang it in a place you will see every day. This will help you to always keep in mind the reasons you want to go to the next level.
- Watch free real estate investor videos online. There are so many videos that give detailed strategies and first steps to real estate investing or a real estate career.
- Sign up for free real estate seminars. Don't go broke purchasing the programs offered at the seminars, just sign

up to get the free information. Learning small bits each day will day will help you grow.

So how likely are you to make $100,000 your first year in real estate? Well that depends on you, your connections, your current knowledge and how much work you're willing to put in. No matter where you are, just get started and be prepared for the Next Level.

Testimonials on Catina's Next Level Coaching Skills

People like Catina because she is REAL. That's rare these days.
James Powell, Licensed R. E. Agent and Mortgage Counselor

Catina took me under her wing as a brand new agent and coached me to my first deal within 30 days of getting my license. I think that speaks volumes about her ability to lead new agents. Catina is a great broker and I am glad I've had the opportunity to work directly with her. She is helping me grow my business daily!
Tiffany Clemons, Licensed Real Estate Agent

Catina stays current with knowledge and is amazing leading new agents in the field. Catina was always there for me, she answered all my questions and helped me close my first deal. Catina also gave me pointers on passing the state exam. She is very professional, punctual, and knows her stuff.
Jill Jones, Licensed Real Estate Agent

Catina is very transparent and genuine when she is discussing real estate sales with new agents. She answers typical questions with much detail and will also use examples from her own professional experiences. Catina is definitely someone who'd be a benefactor to any new agent who is serious about being successful in the business!
Patrick James, Licensed Real Estate Agent

My journey to purchasing a home was educational and life changing. I went in thinking I could just pick a home, make an offer and move in. Silly me! With Catina's skill and professionalism every step of the way, she was able to help me control my emotions and she coached me on what to expect. My home has everything that I wanted. I couldn't be happier.

Yamika Murff, Home Buyer

Catina is by far the best agent in the state. It took 2 months for me to find and close on the perfect home for my family. There are no words that can express my belief and appreciation of her super work. Thanks Catina...you are #1!!!

Dennis Carter, Home Buyer

If you are searching for a realtor you can STOP NOW! Catina is very professional and knows her business inside and out. I interviewed several realtors and largely came away frustrated with a lack of knowledge and professionalism. After speaking with Catina I immediately add the information I needed to make my first purchase being an investment property. I ended up purchasing 2 with Catina and plan to work with her to purchase a primary residence for my own family. Give Catina a call now and you will not be disappointed. Catina is the best.

Alex Hicks, Investor

Catina has an overload of real estate investing advice. She has given me practical wisdom and the support I need to succeed. I love that she holds me accountable and challenges me to go to the next level!

Tiffine Watts, Investor

We are out-state-investors and did not have a local agent. We found Catina through online recommendations and are so grateful to those reviewers who gave her positive comments. Catina goes above and beyond and exceeds expectations. She knows her markets and fights for the best deals for her clients. With our first sale we had problems with our property management company, but Catina was able to smooth out the situation and close a sale in a few weeks. Because of her skill and success, we immediately listed our second property with Catina. We once again had problems with a different property management company and tenant, but once again, Catina's skills coordinated another successful closing within a few weeks.

Catina has a deep pool of contacts and knowledge and we had multiple offers on both properties. We highly recommend her and are forever grateful for her hard-work and friendly, compassionate personality.

Peggy Imanka, Seasoned Investor

I've been working with Catina Willis for almost three years to buy and sell real estate. In that short period of time she has stood head and shoulders above the other realtors I've worked with since I began investing in 2005.

Self-motivated, determined and always accelerating her qualifications. It has been a pleasure to work and prosper with a passionate real estate professional.

Ron Glenn, Seasoned Investor

I am a foreign investor, I live in Argentina, and I am 60 years old, with past experience in real estate investments. When I met Catina for the first time, her smile, her presence and self-assurance, inspired me to believe in her. Time and events showed me that my instincts were right. Catina has helped me purchase quality properties in a very short time. Catina has proven her ability to find good real estate deals. She is concrete, accurate, honest, serious, and very effective, with great ability to overcome unforeseen obstacles. She also has patience and understanding for each of the parties involved. She's a great NEGOTIATOR. In a very short time we have completed many real estate deals together.

It is very important for a foreign investor to have people like Catina when one is so far away. She showed me the best areas to invest. If I had not met Catina, it is very likely that my businesses would not have grown as fast as it did.

Gerardo Martinho, Seasoned Investor

Special Dedication and Acknowledgements

This book is dedicated to all the hard-working real estate agents out there dreaming BIG, hustling, taking brutal beatings, and still getting up each day to do it again.

To the staff, brokers, and agents at my current brokerage, Keller Williams, in Plymouth, MI. This group is truly special and unique. Special dedication to CEO and Team Leader Marybeth Kaljian, Operating Principal Jeff Glover, coach Sherry Swift, and my first real estate coach, John Tenza.

Thanks to my support system, Tiffany Clemons. My good friend of 30+ years Yamika Murff, and especially my son, Mack Arthur Willis III. He's only 16 now, but he is the reason I work relentlessly; he can build on the legacy I'm creating. He says he's getting licensed as a real estate agent as soon as he turns 18. He'll be the youngest face of the Willis Realty Group brand.

Additionally, I need to acknowledge my sister from another mother, Tiffine Watts. She listened to my cries and hugged me through the phone during a very troubling time in my life. Everyone needs a friend like her.

Finally, thanks to my father Jerome Knight and sister Dominique Currie. My mother and brother in heaven Carlene Abraham and Charles Abraham. Last, but not least, I must give thanks and big praise to my awesome GOD.

THANK YOU to all my clients especially those who contributed to the book. Your support is very much appreciated.

About Catina R. Willis, MBA

 Proud mother, real estate leader, and coach. I'm the woman who challenges those around her to go to the next level. My real estate career started in 1997 and my performance and production demonstrate that I aim high and am determined to help others grow. Throughout my career, I've coached dozens of new and seasoned real estate professionals. Also, I've started multiple real estate investment companies, and consistently improved my expertise. Currently, I'm Associate Broker at Keller Williams Realty in Plymouth, MI, and proudly serve on the Agent Leadership Council.

As the founder of Rose Properties Detroit (a property management and investment firm in Detroit). My passion, enthusiasm, and expertise make me so much more than a real estate broker. I support investors from all over the world, providing strategic plans and helping them to acquire and sell properties. My real estate investment journey started in 2001. I've personally bought and flipped 26 properties in Detroit, MI. My philosophy: Learning is a continuous, lifelong experience.

I've been featured on multiple media outlets including: Mlive News, Fox2 Detroit, Detroit Free Press, and WXYZ Detroit ABC 7.

Education and Certifications

- Master's degree of Business Administration in Strategic Management

- Bachelor's degree of Business Administration in Marketing

- Three-time KW Maps BOLD Graduate

- Floyd Wickman Master Sales Coaching and received special recognition for Exceptional Productivity

- Dale Carnegie Coach

- Realcomp Certified Trainer

- Certified Short Sale and Foreclosure specialist

- President and Founder of Rose Properties Detroit - For property management or to buy portfolio investments email catina@rosepropertiesdetroit.com

- President and Founder of Next Level Coaching

For real estate, investment, and business coaching that will take you to the Next Level, visit **Nextlvlcoaching.com or email catina@nextlvlcoaching.com.**